ORVILLE AND WILBUR WRIGHT

DISCOVER THE LIFE OF AN INVENTOR

Ann Gaines

Rourke Publishing LLC
Vero Beach, Florida 32964

www.rourkepublishing.com

PHOTO CREDITS:
©Archive Photos, The Smithsonian Institution, Washington, D.C.

EDITORIAL SERVICES:
Pamela Schroeder

Library of Congress Cataloging-in-Publication Data

Gaines, Ann.
    Orville and Wilbur Wright / Ann Gaines.
        p. cm. — (Discover the life of an inventor)
    Includes bibliographical references and index.
    ISBN 1-58952-121-8
    1. Wright, Orville, 1871-1948—Juvenile literature. 2. Wright, Wilbur,
    1867-1912—Juvenile literature. 3. Aeronautics—United States—
Biography—Juvenile literature. [1.Wright, Orville, 1871-1948. 2. Wright,
Wilbur, 1867-1912. 3.Aeronautics—Biography.] I. Title.

TL540.W7 G27 2001
629.13'092'2—dc21
[B]   2001019375

Printed in the USA

TABLE OF CONTENTS

THE WRIGHT BROTHERS
AND THEIR INVENTION

For thousands of years, people have watched birds and wanted to fly. Wilbur and Orville Wright learned how to do it. They built the first airplane with an engine.

People had flown with **hot air balloons** and **gliders** before. The Wright brothers' machine did not need hot air or wind. Its engine kept it flying.

The Wright brothers built the first airplane with an engine.

THE WRIGHTS LEARN TO MAKE THINGS WORK

Wilbur Wright was born on April 16, 1867. His brother Orville was born on August 19, 1871. Their parents were Susan and Milton Wright. They lived in Dayton, Ohio.

The boys thought their mother could fix anything that was broken. They watched her and learned to take things apart. They liked to figure out how machines worked.

The Wright brothers learned to fix things by watching their mother.

The brothers learned to make bicycles. In 1896, they opened the Wright Cycle Company. They made a bicycle called the Wright Special. They sold Wright Specials for $18 each.

They wanted to make something new. Like many people in the late 1800s, they wanted to invent a flying machine. They watched birds and tried to understand flight.

Many people owned bicycles made by the Wright Cycle Company.

THE FIRST GLIDERS

The Wrights built a glider. It flew like a kite. The brothers could watch it fly. They couldn't steer it, however. It crashed when they tried to make it turn.

They invented a way of steering the glider. Their idea came from watching birds turn in flight. To turn the glider, the Wrights twisted the edges of the wings up or down.

Orville crashes his glider.

In September, 1900, the Wright brothers tested their new glider. They flew it at a windy spot near Kitty Hawk, North Carolina. Wilbur piloted it for a few seconds. The rest of the time the brothers flew it like a kite. Sometimes it soared and turned. Other times it crashed on the sand dunes. The Wright brothers returned to Ohio to make a better glider.

The brothers testing their glider

In July 1901, they came back to Kitty Hawk. Their new glider was stable enough to fly with a **pilot**. Wilbur glided over the beach for more than 300 feet (90 meters). Then he tried to turn the glider. It stopped in the air and fell.

The brothers kept trying. In 1902, they added a special tail to their glider. It kept the glider stable in the air during turns.

The Wright brothers' glider with a pilot

MAKING THE FLYING MACHINE

The Wrights were ready to make a flying machine. They built a plane with two sets of wings, called a **biplane**. It had a gasoline engine on the lower wing. To steer it, the pilot had to lie down on the lower wing. The brothers named their invention "The Flyer."

The Flyer

FLIGHT!

Wilbur won the coin toss to decide who would be the first pilot. On December 14, 1903, he took flight. The engine **stalled**. The plane fell to the ground after only three seconds.

On December 17, 1903, it was Orville's turn. He flew! He stayed in the air for 12 seconds. He flew farther than 100 feet (30 meters). It was the first controlled flight in a plane with an engine.

Over the years Wilbur and Orville crashed many planes.

REMEMBERING THE WRIGHT BROTHERS

The Wright brothers kept making their airplanes better. Soon, they could fly for hundreds of miles. In 1912, Wilbur died. Three years later, Orville sold their airplane company. By the time he died in 1948, people could fly almost anywhere in the world.

People can learn more about the Wrights at the National Air and Space Museum in Washington, D.C., and the Kill Devil Hills National Park in North Carolina.

IMPORTANT DATES TO REMEMBER

1867   Wilbur Wright born (April 16)

1871   Orville Wright born (August 19)

1896   Opened Wright Cycle Company

1900   Tested unmanned glider at Kitty Hawk

1901   Tested manned glider at Kitty Hawk

1903   First controlled flight by a pilot in a
           plane with an engine

1912   Wilbur Wright died (May 30)

1948   Orville Wright died (January 30)

GLOSSARY

biplane (BY playn) — a plane with two sets of wings, one above the other

glider (GLY der) — an airplane without an engine that is kept up in the air by the wind

hot air balloons (HOT AYR beh LOONZ) — huge bags filled with hot air that rise, carrying people in a basket underneath

pilot (PY let) — the person who steers a plane

stalled (STAWLD) — suddenly stopped

INDEX

Further Reading

Beyer, Robert. *Into the Air: The Story of the Wright Brothers and the First Flight*.
    Silver Whistle, 2001.
Freedman, Russell. *The Wright Brothers: How They Invented the Airplane.* Holiday
    House, 1991.

Websites To Visit

•www.gardenofpraise.com/leaders.htm

About The Author

Ann Gaines is the author of many children's nonfiction books. She has also worked
as a researcher in the American Civilization Program at the University of Texas.